# DECOYS

# DECOYS

WILLIAM ROBERTSON

*thistledown press*

Thistledown Press Ltd.
410 2nd Avenue North
Saskatoon, Saskatchewan, S7K 2C3
www.thistledownpress.com

Library and Archives Canada Cataloguing in Publication
Robertson, William B., 1954–, author
Decoys / William Robertson.
Poems.
ISBN 978-1-77187-150-1 (softcover)
I. Title.
PS8585.O322D43 2017 C811'.54 C2017-905321-3

Cover: Decoy carving by Vivian Maxwell; photo by Bill Robertson
Author photo by Shelley Banks
Cover and book design by Jackie Forrie
Printed and bound in Canada

Canada Council for the Arts Conseil des Arts du Canada

Saskatchewan Arts Board

Canada

Thistledown Press gratefully acknowledges the financial assistance of the Canada Council for the Arts, the Saskatchewan Arts Board, and the Government of Canada for its publishing program.

ACKNOWLEGEMENTS

Some of these poems appeared in *The Society* (2011), *Education Matters: The Journal of Teaching and Learning* (2014), *Listening with the Ear of the Heart* (2003). Thanks to the editors of these journals and books. "Sprung" was part of a juried display of poems called 100 Days, 100 Poems at the Saskatoon Public Library in 2006. Yet another valuable thing that libraries do. "For Art, on His Wedding Day" was written for the wedding of Arthur Slade and Brenda Baker and was read at their wedding, Saskatoon, August 1997.

Thanks to the Saskatchewan Writers Guild and its Writing Colonies program, particularly time at St. Peter's Abbey, where some of these poems were written.

Thanks to cabin owners David Carpenter and Honor Kever at Little Bear Lake, the late Vivian Maxwell at Emma Lake, and the late Anne Szumigalski at Turtle Lake. Restorative, inspirational spots kindly lent to me.

I owe a huge debt of thanks to my colleague Artin Lahiji and his two sons Atri and Ix who helped me immeasurably in the IT department. Similar IT thanks go to my pal Rod Macpherson and to my neighbours Mike Harris and his son, William, age ten, who restored my computer files when the device was bombed with an update. Big thanks to readers along the way: my colleague Mika Lafond and my first and best reader, Mary Maxwell. Dave Margoshes was my editor for the press and I couldn't have asked for better: care, respect, an eye for detail, and a sense of humour. Thanks a lot, Dave.

Thanks to the gang at Thistledown Press for responding so positively to the idea of this collection and to the faith they placed in me at the various stages of the publishing process.

In "The Bittern", the lines my mother declaims are from Sir Walter Scott's *The Lady of the Lake*, section XXXI. The italicized lines at the start of "Festive" are from Shakespeare's "Sonnet 18", and the ones part way through "Fly Buzz" are from Emily Dickinson's "465"(J).

CONTENTS

*For Jesse, my son*

*to the memory of my mother-in-law, Vivian Marie (Mitchener) Maxwell (1926-2016), lively companion, voracious reader, astute politico, loving mother-in-law*

*and to the memory of my mother, Ruth Geraldine (Peat) Robertson (1919-2017), wise and gentle guide.*

## DECOYS

The duck, my father many years ago
opined, was indeed a wondrous creature,
flying by air, walking on land,
swimming the sloughs where
he took me, brand new, second-hand
shotgun at the ready to shoot
a few of these peerless morsels,
just a couple of good shots,
some rugged plucking he had
vague memories of doing,
the mysterious gutting,
                    cleaning, drying, stuffing
and roasting best left to my
mother, waiting at home for the men
to return from the hunt
empty-handed, having found no
ducks, all of them too sly to be
shot dead by the likes of us,
no big mallards, canvasbacks, or
redheads, the rapid-thrumming teal.
We saw a couple of dusty
slough hens near an old stone bridge
but couldn't get them to rise.
Wanting still to call this sport,
the old man had me aim the gun
above them as he pelted them
                                        with rocks.

My father had bought his gun
at the local implement dealer,
sent there by men
my father wanted
to be seen with: fishermen,

hunters, curlers, rye-drinkers.
Men who knew what was what.

None of them told my father
where he should hunt. I'm
sure he let them believe
                                        he knew
and we spent the morning driving around
talking of the special qualities
of the amazing bird to be found
nowhere in southwest Saskatchewan but
beneath a defunct bridge where
even a rain of rocks
a threat of hot lead or
perpetual embarrassment
of the hunters being seen
could raise these ducks
                                        to the stubble horizon
a scene from a hunter's calendar
minus the hunters
minus the ducks
just a little down, that day
on their brand-new hunter's luck.

## THE HANTA VIRUS

At this old borrowed cabin, my hosts
have installed a cast-off
TV, black and white, one grainy channel
of CBC, just enough to hear
a farm wife died sweeping up
mouse droppings in a grain bin.

When we force the door
of the garage cum boathouse
with its leaky canoe, crazy tools,
and milk cartons of old records, my son
spots his new treasure, fishing lures
in tangles of line, curled leaders
nestled in thousands of tiny turds.

I tell him just to back away, forget them,
close the door. We've got tackle
boxes full of every lure he could need.
I've caught twenty fish already this trip
on the same lure. His look tells me
he could never be so dull and no matter
what I say about this mysterious virus
I find him just stepping in from
a walk every time I emerge from a nap
or shower, him brushing his hands
on his shorts, saying he needed air.

When I find the pile of lures at the side
of the cabin, having gotten up sooner
than either of us expected, I tell him
I'm not a doctor or a disease expert,
I don't know enough about the damn
virus to know whether these turds,
the ones all over the garage, could
cause him to get sick. The odds are

against it, I suppose, but what should I do,
I ask him. He hasn't a clue. Shrugs
to tell me so. So we wash the lures,
I make him wash his hands, don't
even bother to tell him I should
kick his ass, don't know whether
I'm doing the right thing or not,
just know if I let him weasel
through that garage, dragging out
the lure he thinks is perfect
for the biggest fish, the kid could
get sick, could die, then I'd have
to say I tried, or I didn't know,
what that farm family is likely saying
right now: he was young, he wanted
something big. I tried. I didn't know.

## JUST LIKE

As children, year after year
fooled by our schoolbooks,
we ran outside into winter
to build snowmen, snow forts,
have snowball fights, disappointed
always with the dry prairie stuff
that crumbled in our hands. I remember
someone's parent dropping us off
at the edge of a slough where we
tied on our skates in the 20 below,
spent most of our warmth and strength
shovelling off a patch of ice rippled
frozen by the wind, slapped our puck
at each other till it careened
into a drift and we dug for it
till our ride came, home with numb
feet and hands, nothing like
the books we read, the shows
we watched, radio
grimly announcing another part
of our grim mythology, some fool motorist
chanced a walk from his stuck vehicle
to a nearby farmhouse light, died halfway,
found stiff as a fencepost.

In July's holiday on Turtle Lake
my young son wants to catch all
the fish he's seen in magazines.
I tell him those
are American magazines, there are no
bass here, no blue gill, catfish, crappies,
nothing for most of the exotic lures
he's bought with his birthday money.
I tell him about the Indigenous guides

north of La Ronge who keep the lightest
tackle boxes on the lakes: knife, pair of pliers,
some leaders, jigs, red and whites.
The boy's not impressed, I see
him putting on the old cynicism,
staring glumly at summer Saskatchewan,
two months of nothing like
the fishing shows on TV, till he
brightens at the sight of some bird
with a fish in its claws.
That's an osprey, I tell him, fish hawk,
the fish at least a pound,
the scene he recognizes well
from the ten dollar bill we paddle home
to unfold and see. By nightfall's
campfire he's roasting marshmallows
in a wind that showers him
with sparks, but never mind, he's still
talking about the bird
with the fish that's just like
all the pictures he's seen.

## WART

I told him I got it
from holding a toad too long
but my son didn't believe me,
told me that was just a story,
spent the rest of the summer warning me
away from frogs

Finally caught the thing
on the hard denim edge
of a pocket,
decided I'd get it burned off.
Liquid nitrogen on a Q-tip,
the doctor said that
should do it, watched it
fall off my finger like
a little red lentil,
three or four tiny roots
still grasping at sky.
I told my son they cried
for another wart,
another joke, but in the night
the side of my hand like fire
I reached for the cool touch
of the toad,
the sight of my son smiling
like a sunbeam
seeking it out in the yard.

## THE SNAPPER

A clutch of viewers
at Wilson's Shell, we stood
round the washtub of dirty water
that held the snapping turtle
a big guy named Butts
carried up from the river,
telling us between long drags
not to dangle a digit or any
other thing we didn't want
snapped off over the son
of a bitch, it almost took his hand,
he said, the way its grim head
with Grandpa's smile could jerk
right around and take you

He was sixteen and smoked, didn't
go to school, telling this to men
and me, a child, without my friends,
there by luck or accident to hear
him swear, watch him do something
dangerous, foolhardy, tell a story
then bum a smoke from other men.

## FULL GROWN

Outside the far window
a wheeling flock of geese, April,
and the sun mixes with snow and rain.
They've paired up, mated, by summer
the goslings will be walking a foot tall
on the river island. By fall
they'll be flying south, looking full grown,
facing the distance, the guns.

My students all look full grown
though they forget their pens, pencils,
tissues for runny noses, cough
into the general air and ask again
what time it is.
Some have fallen to the side already —
there's nothing like the gaggle that crowded
my room in September, food brought
to them with the fun. Now the sun
of April changes again to snow
and a biting north wind. It's nasty
out there and the geese, far out
that window, are getting ready to bring
their young into this world.

They don't have long to get them grown,
those geese. One student rubs her nose
down her sleeve. Her mother would cringe
if she could see. But she can't.
Her young has flown off over
the trees, the wind is strong,
and in the pits below, the hunters have loaded
their guns.

## SPRING FINALS

Inside the college building
students are writing
their first year English final.
Six were late, two showed up
without a pen, one didn't
show up at all, one just ran
out the door to answer her phone.
Her mother's in ICU. The two
pregnant women are careful as
they lower themselves to sit.

Over the soccer pitch snow
turns from lazy flakes to downright
spring storm.  Robins, thirty of them,
red breasts puffed with lust,
make wild runs at one another
while off to the side Bohemian waxwings
gorge on last year's crabapples.

Everything is right
on schedule.

ARBUTUS

I hitchhiked to the coast
not specifically, but
with an addled certainty
I'd sit beneath an arbutus tree,
watch the waves wash
my romantic soul
trying to make love to Joni Mitchell
lyrics about an arbutus tree

found one on a hippie island,
no less, purposely
missed the ferry (knew
there'd be another)
sat beneath it as the waves
washed the stones with
a satisfying rush that had nothing
or possibly everything to do
with my young heart

drove to the coast a few years later
with a roommate who
claimed we'd cast off work
with fishing and drinking,
drank and fished to the same
island, same arbutus tree
he mispronounced, hilariously,
when he asked why I laughed
I said it was me
this whole tree thing is about
how funny I can be

## EMERGING

What's with this green pillowing
out of the trees like foamy shave
cream cutting off my view
of the girl going by on the street
in her shades, even on cloudy days?
I liked that, up my alley
and past my house she came —
chin cocked like a brave
little bantam she walked
past my gaze, but now
the lilacs lap the window like
goofy dogs, the crabapple tree
so full of pink I can't think bird
or bee. Winter's been a cold
prison of shitty food so long
it's like being sat down to a good
steak and bottle of wine, my stomach
can't take it, I get sick, want
to go back to my basement with
the 60-watt light, the heavy quilts
pressing down like 40 degrees
below of snow on the car that wouldn't
start for three months, ran rough
the other five — and now I'm
supposed to be happy to be alive,
dance near naked on the grass
that's already over my ankles,
the dandelions, the cottonwood sticky
bud cases stuck to my feet. I
face the springtime in Saskatchewan
three months late, it's too much,
it's fuckin' great

## SPRUNG

Here comes that great uneven V
as Spring honks down the sky
calling calling up above,
lighting a match under every
young dog left in its mushy yard

what the geese must see
from overhead,
silly little mutts leaping
from the lawns

old dogs not fooled by this trick
lying muzzle down on their paws.

I hear this conversation coming closer,
then my neighbour's dog explodes
as the honkers creak over the house.

Oh, the times I've wanted to shoot
that dog, the times I've shot at geese.

Is it jealous we are
they get to leave, angry as young dogs
when they take away the light?
We leap from our chairs,
welcome the sight.

## SPEAKING OF RHUBARB

a stand in every alley
blueberries after a burn
Saskatoons by the river
blackberries out on the coast

indigenous plants
poor man's food smacks
the secretary, folding
her arms, putting paid
to that conversation, we
nod at our coffees

a few more pie triumphs
a few more stories of growing
up stretched for a pail
of crabapples, a bag
of frozen berries, a bunch
of rhubarb the missus doesn't need
thought you could use it
no trouble at all

ducking out on a thank-you
a few more mouths to feed

poor man's food
we nod.

## THE FLOWERS OF CANADA

*for Liz Philips*

Dad said it would be an adventure,
or maybe it was Mom, anyway
the little wheels on the utility trailer
Dad built spun three times as fast
as those on the Merc as we bulled
our way west, Dad making miles, through
the Laurentians and around Superior.
My comics ran out.
Betty's ran out.
Janet's were for babies. Mom
pulled out the flower cards I'd gotten
for a birthday from a well-meaning soul,
had never looked at. Oh, come on,
she said, and started flashing them.

By the time we'd cleared Saskatchewan
and Dad, cigarettes in a steady cloud,
was eyeing up the Rockies' peaks, we could

rattle off Prairie Lily (Saskatchewan), Wild Rose
(where we are now), Trillium (where we used
to live), Dogwood (your new provincial flower, her
eyes glittering, getting back to where she
was from, what Dad had promised her years
before), Showy Ladies Slipper, Jack-in-the-Pulpit,
Fringed Gentian, you say, now we're out
for a walk, I used to know them all.

Never saw them in the field, save what Mom
could point at, but for one summer, one
great burst of journey with destination
on our minds, I knew them by province,
by size and colour, by each unbelievable
name. Let you show me the couple

we come across, tell you
of my father, with distance and safety
fretting his brow, of my mother handing out
sandwiches, leading us down to the bog
to see marigolds growing wild, my father,
with a cigarette, big trucks a blur
behind him, calling us back, my mother not
letting us pick them, just standing still
for this bright and orange
minute.

## MATING

A full moon up over
the trees to the southwest

In the spring stubble, Canada
geese and cranes exchange news

In the creek, birds I'll probably
never name explain their desire

I've phoned home. My wife tells me
our son has a convoluted tale

of four trips to the hospital, blacking
out, life in a trailer with two kids not

getting any easier. I sit in the dark
watching the moon so strong and silent

over all this mating

GEO

How many years
      were you there?
top of your mountain
beside your ocean

I picked you up
   round  speckled
   red in the river
   flat as prairie

You sit on my windowsill
now:  French vineyard
         Australian sea
         Hawaiian volcano
came back with me
in my suitcase

Anne said certainly
rocks move, just
more slowly than we
care to watch
and when they want

You're looking out my window
at my small walled yard:
bricks you know
glass you know

      know you've got time
      where you're from
      where you can go
      how you'll roll

## FLY BUZZ

What does the fly know, anyway?

It walks something it can't see
buzzing occasionally
to distract me from my work

I take another swing at it
rolled up newspaper
riles it to another window
where it continues its tiny
fly-brained inquiry
with the impossible outside
walking again *with blue*
*uncertain stumbling buzz*
up my front window

perched on its invisible prison
wall it walks what it knows
is light, I can't explain
glass to a fly, can't explain
window, go about
my work till the next frantic
buzz springs me from my seat

## HOLDING THE HOME

The wasps build homes in holes
in the stucco buzz
about the children as they play

In front of the house crows attack
the cat, three forms of black
tumble, caw, cry out

Standing beneath the tree at evening
I hear the green, being eaten
away, sticky caterpillars drop
on plastic thread to mess
our clothes and hair

We are not living in a movie
We are not living so far
in the country as to keep
guns at the door for the bear

We live in the city
on either side houses
are renewed,
eavestroughers, roofers
clatter and scrape
tapping back into shape
these failing organisms,
these houses full of life

buzzing and cawing, tearing
us down, and some of it guards
the door, broom held high
chasing off the black
falling from the sky

## STARTING THE STORY

I need to know someone
was watching me today.
Not like an angel, though
that would have helped,
but someone who needed a laugh,
someone with a sense of humour,
my youngest son, or the son
whose house I just left,
him and his bright university pals
watching me out the window as I
headed down the alley, the archetypal
comedy prop lying there, wasp's nest
with the leafy branch through it
blown down by the wind, and I,
curious as always — how many of those things
have I brought home after all — seeing no wasps
deciding to pick it up by the branch
then exactly what's supposed to happen
when the guy pokes a wasp's nest: out
they come and me in floppy sandals on gravel
thinking I can outrun wasps,
wrenching my lower back, swatting

at hot pokers sticking me behind
the right knee, hopping and howling
holding my back, my leg, the rest
of the afternoon laid up on
anti-inflammatory drugs and an ice pack thinking
please God, hear my prayer: let someone

have been there, some kid especially who
needed to learn cartoons don't just happen,
jokes really do have a goat, that stupid guy
who walks up to the bear's cave, a dud
firecracker, a wasp's nest, looking
for answers, looking
to start a story.

## THE BULL

As we descend the Bench,
last of the Cypress Hills
to Gull Lake and the # 1 Highway,
I remark upon the vista
to my daughter, granddaughters all
too numbed by screens
in their laps to glance, the land
stretching out, millions of years
of water, ice, stones, scouring
Saskatchewan to grass, grazing
land covered by cows, calves, donkeys
pumping oil from the ground.

I must be getting old — *am* old —
this view I've seen a thousand times:
Gull Lake, the grass in all its greens,
that bull, sequestered from the rest,
not even chewing, not really looking,
lying like the lion of the world
watching Gull Lake as I do
but without hurry, worried
that something's being missed
its massive assurance that all —
as I rush by —
is what is.

## TAXONOMY

The bush country is waiting
like a promise it's kept
for its daughter to come back
from school. Everything is perfect,
ordinary as it always was.
She's learned new names
for old things. Tells her uncle
there's not a pickerel in a single
one of these lakes when he holds
a big one up for her to see,
says it's walleye, call it walleye
the way a professor corrected her
down at the university, she'd never
in her life heard anyone use so much
conviction as this man, almost angry,
she thought he was, and never
on a single Saskatchewan lake
like the one her uncle's just come off,
lived beside all his life, rod in one hand,
pickerel in the other, wiping the smile
off his face with her word, walleye
she tells him, use the proper word,
and feels the first little hurt
of loneliness she makes for herself
coming home with new names
to push her people away.

## BUSH LEAGUE ADAM

Time was, birds were all just birds
undifferentiated animals that flew and made
noise above till someone had to name them:
    fish catcher
    big black bird
    seed cracker
    seed cracker with white stripe

The fall migration sweeps over my inlaws' cabin.
I pivot on my heels, head stretched back to catch them all
with my categorizing gaze, a walk no longer
just a walk with the creatures of the sky and bush:
there's the raven who will stay all winter,
the chickadees, black-capped, too. Those
are juncos travelling through and high above
the noisy geese. Is that a ruby-crowned kinglet?
That a western pee wee? I'm dizzy
with this turning beneath the trees, a modern Adam
with binoculars and book trying hard
to name them all, as if the grouse's gray or rufous form
changes how that grouse gathers its food,
picks up bits of rock on the road
to help it grind its feed.

And yet, no longer a child content with merely bird,
I respect the minutia of their difference
from themselves, most notably from me,
stuck clumsily here beneath them, each step prompting
a flurry in the branches as they show me, briefly,
their wings, those beaks, vastly important to them
whether they choose the berry
or the seed.

ANY TREE

The clay-coloured sparrow and the house wren
send me news from their trees:
an insect buzz, the liquid tying
of grassy ribbon, these voices
mix with the ticking my car
makes cooling at highway's edge.
            Somewhere up ahead there's construction
though all we can see is a young man
with a red sign, stock still, in the middle of the road,
a line of us dutifully pulled over waiting.

Call after call comes from those trees
that once enclosed a house, some buildings,
a farm gone back to ground, the trees still
hanging on to their human roots, planted
by hand against the long view of open ground.

Because there's a wren in our back yard
a clay-coloured sparrow three doors down
migrants who return each year,
I believe these cousins call to me, sitting here
patiently with my windows open to the heat,
believe their lives are focused on the farmer's
trees, their windbreak, their screen, defense
against the sky and winter's nineteen weeks,
but I could be wrong
                                        they don't sing
those heady declarations, those intricate loops
to me at all, or any farm wife who ever
watered some precious sticks to life.

These are trees, this is grass and sky.
The people all obey some bored guy
with a sign by the side of some
black strip that's hard, often noisy,

and goes on over the hill. The birds
are birds like they were a thousand
years ago, calling *my tree* to one
another, though, depending on the season,
any tree, however it got there, will do.

## THE BIG NOISE

The outrage of the community
centres on young people let loose
from school, drinking, smoking, swearing
so we can hear, oh yes,
every fearless word of it.

Whether the white-crowned sparrow
notices or not, he, yes, it's a he,
wants the neighbourhood to know
this is his territory, the house
finch a half-block away, the robins
skirling by, the crows in the big spruce
scolding the youngsters and their liquor,
or maybe they're encouraging them,
it's hard to tell when I'm tired.
I just want to sleep.
The grad party won't let me.

And the white-crowned sparrow, king
of the neighbourhood, will sing
the light away and every noisy teen
under the table. As long as no other
sparrow, or red-headed finch, for that matter,
moves in on the big noise
he's making tonight.

— *Burnaby*

## WARBLER

This alley the worst eyesore
in the neighbourhood. Outside the rickety
red fence, unpainted for years, the weeds
and long grasses try their best
to hide the garbage — tin cans,
drink containers, musty newsprint —
but give up and tumble in long hanks
into each other's dusty arms.

Lighting on the fence, the yellow
warbler flicks his black eye on me, drops
to the grasses to hop
like a cricket, some jumping insect,
from chicken bucket to tampon box,
his yellow the only yellow in this world
or any other on this clouded-over day.

I stand where I usually walk quickly,
watch him work his warbler labour
through each bit of grass, each weed,
ask it, why aren't you in the top
of the elm trees? It glances me
its improbable reply, flies away,
small stroke of lightning
on a dreary day.

## SUCCESS

Hopping along the sidewalk
under overhanging bumpers,
Range Rovers, BMWs, big
Silverado 4 x 4s, house
sparrows check
the grillwork, radiators, even
tire treads for anything
they can take to the nest
they've managed to build
in the place the soffit blew
apart above the entrance
to the real estate office.

Hardy beasts, as the Jaguars,
Mustangs, big Rams
roll up, they dodge the wheels,
the Italian shoes, get to work
being the best scavenger
this multi-acre field
of asphalt and steel can put up.

Their wild cousins
in the disappearing pastures
outside the rampant city
give way to development
— the real estate craze —
die back south year by year
  giving ground
to adaptable breeds
in concrete fields.

## JUST SPARROWS

I know how many more
house sparrows we have
than robins, warblers, jays.
Hear them in every bush and tree
scolding, singing, their raucous
parliaments spilling into the street.
Have heard the ornithologists
scoff at what the merlin takes.
Know my Darwin, know the numbers
know exactly what colour Nature is
in beak and little claw. But
I can't help hating the crow
this morning in its black calculation,
moving from pole to wire to limb
amidst a growing concentration
of sparrows watching it steal
one of their young, back to pole
for a surer grasp, off quietly
down the lane, the little life
in its beak assuredly passed, the many
sparrows aquiver with their version
of horror, frustration, entirely
unfamiliar in their tiny bird brains
with how many of their babies
they can afford to lose.

## GOLDFINCHES AGAIN

*for John Clark*

He can't move off the porch, or could,
if his house was on fire, but
he sits with a cigar in his hand,
a cane laid out on either side of him,
asks me what's making that song,
right now, above us in the tree.

I range out from the steps,
binoculars at the ready, following
the sweet loop of song behind
the leaves, him asking me, gruff
behind his smoke, what, what
is it? and I spot it, feed him
what he wants but can't
hop up and see: yellow, mostly yellow,
I tell him, a black face, black wings
with some white in them.

A goldfinch, he crows, I had goldfinches
last year, they must be back,
but I'm cautious, looks bigger
than a goldfinch, and we make the joke
about small things looking bigger.
But I'm looking up, not down, I say.

I follow it around the house, leaving
him sitting there, weighed down by age, ill
health, bad luck, calling
to me, do you still see him, but
I've scared it off.

We used to walk to town and back
three miles each way from a school
we worked together, him waving

his walking stick like a pointer
at that mallard, that kingbird, swearing
a blue jacket of words for every man
that did him wrong, but the birds
were good, green head or red winged,
the birds just sang the songs we worked
to put words to, him swearing at me now,
well, was it a goldfinch or not?

Sure, I tell him, sure it was, you've
got goldfinches again.

## CAT + SQUIRREL

one on the fence
one on the ground
one too smart
to get caught
other too smart
to try
giving each other
the careful eye
tails flick-flicking
with that careful eye
that possible
vaguely possible
try

## EMMA LAKE TRIO

Juncos in the neighbours' trees
dart among the falling leaves
soon the season darkens down
to raven and to me

Raven at the top of the tallest tree
croaks its presence as I wander in
without my key
Trying the bathroom window I
tumble and bleed
Wingbeats of raven tell me
it's seen all it needs to see

Ruffed grouse leads its perfect
rusty brown and black fan
out of the spruce, through the ditch
up on the road where
it cocks its head quizzically
at my approach. On a hunting day
I'd have popped it by now
but this is a teaching day.
I school myself all over again,
its shape, its colour
its brave march

## RUBY-THROAT

The ruby-throated hummingbird has built
her cup of lichen twenty feet
above the busy yard where we
plant and water and mow and shout.
We watch her needle beak,
her stab of tail,
her fidelity to the two white eggs
we know are in that lichen nest

The crafty raven slides its black
shadow across the yard, the hungry
merlin shrieks its clear intentions
to the road while children enact
the cruelties of their parents
in simple wars of stones and arrows.

The tiny mother has flown across the Gulf
of Mexico and half of North America
to sit right here, buzzes out of her nest
in view of us all, if we care to look,
then buzzes back.
The neighbour's dog
erupts in a spasm of fearful barking,
the jet-skis have taken over the lake,
a dump truck bellows great gouts
of smoke as it roars to a new cabin site
and the little bird hums past
my head to its nest, strong
as the tree in which she's hidden,
frail as the nest anyone
could miss.

## DEAD CLOWN

Belly up on the boulevard, how
did you fall? Such a small
body, really, in your large cloak
of fans and dusters, every tourist
cawing delight at your gaudy yak
yak all over town, your sweeping black
and white gown. Someone
must have decided, a quick
decision, too, you were one
too many and drove you down. Who's
to say you were the one to go? Who
decides? But there you lie
with the few bugs fall can muster
feasting you on your bed
of withered leaves. No forty below
for you, the one thing I can count on
as I wallow my way through deep
snow to school, your willingness to play
the fool in your all-weather call
and call, dipping down just
before me, hopping away free.
No winter, no spring, removed
from it all. How seldom
we see you fall, fallen now,
stretched out in your funeral suit
so distinguished in repose, and up
the street a tree full of your gang
heckling another passerby,
dancing before a car.

## DOWNED

The little woodpecker has gathered
all its quick colours together
for the night, its black and white ladder-
back, red head and throat, even
that delicate yellow belly you'd call white
if you saw it in the tree making
that sharp whistle it does, making
its jump from branch to branch, making
those holes you spot later but hear
only occasionally as a tap-tap-tap you
turn round and round below to find
but don't, dizzy in front of puzzled
heavy pedestrians, but now
you see them clearly, those colours
hanging limp from your hand, the sharp
wood-piercing beak bouncing elastically
at the alley where you found it quite
by accident, quite intact, unable
to leave it you carry it carefully
by its wingtips trying hard to think
beyond the amazing stillness of its colours
what you'll tell your wife when she meets
you at the door to ask why
and you hold it up to her like a gift
you're convinced she'll receive.

## AUGUST'S GRAVITY

Walking home in early evening I see
in unkind relief dragonfly
on pavement stranded by season's
end flopping helplessly

finger to its searching legs it clings so
I can hold it upright, survivor
from the times of Tyrannosaurus
unable to last much beyond
the first frost it attempts
an escape but cannot overcome
late August's gravity.

Picking it up again I cup it
from the breeze so this fierce navigator
of summer gardens can endure
the indignity of my hot breath
the way home to my young son
who will shriek, try to hold it.

Sensing this final humiliation
it gathers its memories
of mid-summer air, rises
on invisible wings, leaving me
heavy and human on the sidewalk
staring it to a speck in the darkening blue.

## BEFORE WINTER

Late September at your parents' cabin, gold
coins of birch and aspen piled on the road,
the lanes, spilling in the door
with the changing breeze. The impossibility
of saving them, though, year after year,
we both pick handfuls to be forgotten,
crinkling in a corner. On the shelf upstairs,
your dead brother's football trophies. The bad
story of drugs. His promise. How
he might have made something of the sport.
We both know such making it
consists of more than one good season.
My daughter, who must have been eyed over
by the other girls in her school as so and so much
competition. Me driving all over the city
to her games. The basketball coach telling me
she'd be on the senior team a year early. Then
the game I came to and she wasn't there. Her teammates
looking round at me from the bench, thinking
they were surreptitious, knowing where she was,
that she was one less they'd have to practise hard,
get up every day, fight fight fight for three more years
to beat.

It's been years since university.
How were we ranked and who's come first?
I know my time there was frantic and flaws
flaws and going on anyway. Teaching,
quitting teaching, teaching again, who's
to say what's first but that we gather
the gold coins every year, talk about the ones
who fell, the ones who got up again, make a promise,
this year, to press the leaves between sheets
of wax paper, trying with such frail human
hope to hold this short shimmering season.

## SUMMER'S LEASE

Gundersons' snow shovel's still
on their porch, and the rain's
been so heavy Jim can't
get any blueberries in.
Labour Day weekend's coming up
and my bathing suit's still on
the peg by the back door. I look
across at Allan's place to see
the few jobs he's been able
to get to this year, notice
a couple of yellow leaves fall.
I want to call, Allan, drop
that hammer and put those leaves
back up. Drop
whatever you're doing, Allan,
and nail those damn leaves
back up.

## THE WAY THE LEAVES FALL

Leaves fall on Clint's new
grave. I remember
I wanted to hold onto fall
the year I left school,
watch the leaves go and try
to catch them, buy
pencil crayons, fresh notebooks, not
go to school, step out of things
starting and watch the way
the year ends, life closes down,
the way the leaves fall
on my friend's new place.

## FATTEN OR FLEE

Ice shillies against itself as it forms
along the edge of the lake. Out in the bay
a pair of black ducks laugh at the long row
of geese crying at one another to rise,
stay in line, bank south to leave.
On the far side of the water someone's
hammering the last of fall into place, the storm
of two days ago having thrown branches across
the roads and reminded him to prepare,
prepare. The ducks laugh at him, too.
They don't have long to laugh. Raven
knows this, pinions sounding *wha wha*
as it surveys the country that will soon revert
to it and those chickadees back in the trees,
too busy nearly to notice the season.
Two days ago
a nuthatch on the step sat stunned as if
it had hit the window. I bent to it
and off it flew, just resting or
looking for a new way to be
eaten, but now it's found its way
straight to the bush.

Across the lake a pair of coyotes
fight, or maybe that's a dog
they're marauding, yowling about being
a victim. Raven goes by again, dark
in the darkening day, *wha wha*
watching over the chattering lake as it
gobbles itself, fighting for the last bits
to eat.

## ONE LAMP

Muskrat runs a quiet zipper
across the cold lake
closing in its fish for the night.
Above, the geese, some cranes,
ducks gadding about around the bend,
in the distance, coyotes letting us know
the nature of the universe is darkness,
that sickle moon scooping up
all the light we'll have till morning
frost-ridden and so aware of winter.
Behind me, where I'll never find it,
an owl warns the mice it's coming,
tumbles from its tree on wings
quiet as an untouched razor,
unlike this trio of ducks winging it
hard to join their fellows, pinions
creaking me off my bench
up the path to the one lamp
I left on. Back to work.
In the morning, all the fish
safe, from me anyway, and the ice
getting ready to change everything
again.

## THE FEET UP

The woods hereabouts are full
of rabbits, two just scooted through
the yard, both of them turning
white from the feet up, getting ready
for what's soon to come

They don't care about their mottled
appearance, where it starts or
how it ends, as long as in summer
they're just a noise in the bush,
in winter a streak across snow.

It's hard enough being a rabbit,
nerved and jumpy, as they are,
foxes following close behind,
wolves as wise as their hunger
is sharp.

Rabbits don't spend their quick time
worrying about white, trust
it like I trust the dawn, having
trained myself to sleep through
the darkest hour, then shave
with the bright light on.

— *Emma Lake*

## FESTIVE

Yes, *rough winds do shake*
*the darling buds of* May, but
in their place, it being late October,
I've strung the bare yard's birches
with chickadees topsy-turvying their way
over every shaking branch, buzzing
their fat little black and white heads
at one another, a rambunctiously alive
set of festive lights that blink beautifully
off at sundown, start up again before
I step outside to warm up the van.

And what do I pay them
                                        for my pleasure?
A handful of seeds from a bag
inside the door, a quiet blessing
each time I pass beneath them, rarely
stopping, rarely intruding on their songs,
this keeps them happy and working
the way I keep moving right along.

## SAINTHOOD

*for Mary*

Let's all be saints in this morning
light as the days on days of dull sky
turn to sun and we walk from snowy meadow
to snowy spruce, the paths kicked up
before us by the deer, each of us stopping
stock still, palms outstretched and full
of seed for the little balls of chickadee-
dee-dee who take forty seconds to get to know us
then drop from the branches to clutch for
seconds a finger, lift a seed, and go.

Let's be St. Francises all, lover
of birds and the sky, your form
an angel's silhouette against the sun
where the path leads out of the trees
your hand high, feathered ball of trust in your palm
and the little laugh in your throat,
what God saved for you when you grew
impatient with being a child.

*— St. Peter's Abbey, Muenster*

## WHITE ON WHITE

If the owl on the pole outside Warman, Sask.
has any uncertainties about the thing just pulled up
to stare, it budges nothing
but its round white head

stares right back its Asian gaze
neutralizing the negative charge
on everything I thought important

till now in this landscape of snow and owl. My full
awareness becomes its little hooked beak
razor claws, perfect designs for doing exactly
what it does, serrated feathers, eyes
that stare from the center of the cold that kills
us hurrying by in our machines, each
with a prayer we rarely say for no
breakdown, no walk in the snow.

I stop, open my window, remove
my dark glasses, give myself anxiously
through my eyes. Owl from the snow
country gives me its gaze,
saves all of itself for itself,
its beautiful sure self.

## YOUR STRING

Black kite on a white world,
what holds your string?
your shadow on the iced river

the one thing strong enough
to soar against the cold
that holds us against our windows
blue sky stretched so thin
it will shatter bone
china slivers around us
as snow over town
over blue brown of trees
above them all
Raven
creating its breeze

## DELECTABLE

A frozen river the snowmobiles
have run up and down like lines
on paper, six, now seven
ravens chasing one another up
and down the scale of winter

bunched in a chord, strung out
in icy notes beneath the blue opera
dome of this lasting season, oh
for such a black-swirling cacophony
that we'll riot to our own Rite
of Spring, burst out of doors
to watch our river crack open,
spill itself along all those lines,
give the ravens something delectable
for such a scintillating performance

## RAVEN ON FROZEN RIVER

a comma

what's before?

what's after?

when Flaubert spent his morning
putting you in, his afternoon
taking you out, was his page
this white or
had he been here before?

now you jump

a pause, a pause again
                                        a list perhaps
I could spend all day
watching you divide
snowy silence
from itself

a pause    another pause

the entire unknowable danger
marked into common fragments
by you my valuable friend
pushing my day further
from its dark end

— *Prince Albert*

## CALL OF THE NORTH

A dog on each of the boats
rounding the point sets off
the husky on the island, all three
raring to get at each other, drowning
out the cry of the loon, one only,
bobbing against an outcrop,
all of them lost to the gale
of the Twin Otter roaring off
Yellowknife Bay out over
                                        the darkening lake.

## ANOTHER ONE ABOUT THE DOG IN THE NIGHT

The dog's brain isn't big enough
to invent death and God so
it barks at the dark all night.

I can't sleep so I blame the dog
when it's death and the dark
at fault. My brain's big enough
to invent God, too, and that's
what's kept me from barking,
lying here, not sleeping,
with nothing else to do.

— *San Miguel de Allende*

## DOGS OFF CHAINS

A rare sunny day on the autumn beach,
pretty women in bright clothes
slip their dogs from their chains,
throw balls and sticks at the waves.
Happy, healthy dogs exhilarate
in the warmth, the wet, the women
love them, call Brutus, call Dingo, call
Rags, everyone passing in happy barks
and hellos when one black and white bolt
lightnings the accommodating sand
teeth first into the side
of a polite dog on a chain, Fang's woman
screaming its name. It does not obey.
Again it plunges its snout into the terrified
underside, its owner calling, the attacker's
owner screaming as she runs, as
another dog enters the fray, three
shouting women pulling apart
their dogs, crying, pleading, other women
up and down the beach giving commands
re-fastening chains. The three
back away from one another, too busy
to offer apologies, accusations,
asking their dogs why, as they yank
their chains, why doggie, why
did you do such a bad, bad thing.

— *Adelaide*

## THE WOODS

In Gros Morne we ask the guide
about bears. Not a problem. Moose?
Not a problem, either. Just use
common sense. With our binoculars
we stalk the warblers, the thrush,
the white-throated sparrow, scare up
a flock of eiders on the river, send
a drumming grouse over a ridge
for cover. The squirrels give us loud
rapid lectures on property rights, but
we thud by, completely uninterested.

I turn to a new call, my wife
grabs my arm, there, she says,
and the black smoke
of an animal — dog size, coyote size,
wolf size — drifts from bush to bush
across our path, there and gone.
Twenty yards ahead, fresh canine
scat on the trail, not its trail, but
our one way out, the way
we came, the way ahead. How
exciting, we remark, the forced smile
the quick step to the car.

## NOT SAYING A WORD

we're okay,
the car's okay, a crack
low on the bumper, but
you can hardly tell
the moose got up, shook
itself, dragged its leg
into the bush

probably trailing
a coyote or two by now, a fine
edge to their patience
quietly watching
their kill, just one
of thousands on this island
after all, some local guys
tell me, and the car's
a rental so don't worry
don't even say a word

— *Port au Choix, Nfld.*

## RUNNING TO THE CAPELIN

Just watch me lift a thousand gulls
with a single bound down
from the car across the sand
to stand with the little fishes
flopping away their life
their spawn then gone
down the gullet of the herring gull
black-backed gull glaucous gull
lifting through the rain the fog as I
leap boulders leap logs
scoop a dozen and run back
to the road to my wife

we've miles to go
in the sluicing rain
but the capelin are running
I can catch fish
raise gulls
with my bare hands

*— Badger, Nfld.*

## BROOK TROUT

This fish wasn't even going to be interested
in what I was throwing at it,
fifteen casts at least into a hole
below a fallen log on this willow-
choked stream before I saw it
move, thirty more before my cheap flashy
spoon crossing and crossing its quiet
morning finally irritated it
into snapping the stupid morsel
that pulls back, pulls back hard
up and down on the water it
whacks its silver and I want to call
my friends downstream but scared it will
get off before they get here, hold
the line pulling back faster than I
can reel it in, trying to adjust the drag
while reeling, the fish boiling its water
whips the rod tip still gaining on line till
I grab the reel still and back away
from the water, hit a tree, hit
the embankment, kick backwards up the slope,
the waist of my jeans scooping gobs
of dirt, pockets full, backing through saplings
snapping my neck, my arms, the line
holding, fish still slapping the water
rocks, sand, dirt
the grass in front of me, I fall
before it, muddy bloody crazy
both worn out, I rub away the muck
to shine its silver, its glowing red
spots ignite the dry grass
I call loud, call hard
the fire it's started.

— *White Gull Creek*

## BONE CREEK BROWN

In a messy stretch of green bottomland
in the round hills west of town
where the creek gathers speed in spring,
plunges across its curves
and froths in its corners,
I sent a little fly tied
to my long length of line
into a hole the red willow
bows over, just threw it
at the current and sent it down,
the wind clattering budding branches
around me, spring sleet smacking
my ruddy cheeks, and the creek
grabbing my little drab green fly, sluicing it
into itself and beneath the froth,
the jouncing gather of sticks and reeds
to where the brown trout lives
and gathers its meals with the long
curved hook of its quick sharp jaw.

The wind, the sleet, the rain
on my glasses, no room to cast,
small trees crowded round and bent
with wind, with flood debris,
such a suck of mud up against them
and my fly in the wind, I lay it
straight on the surface of the stream
send out the line, again and again,
and the brown trout, dark at its spine
then bronzing to amber belly
where red spots gather like drops of wild
splattered blood, the big brown that quietly
commands this stretch of creek, the brown
lunges from its hole for my fly

so small, so sharp the hook that takes
the cartilage that edges its mouth
and we fight

                    my rod wows, my reel
shrieks with the wind through the coulee
and the huge brown trout that owns
this water, owns its frogs, its minnows,
owns its water voles and mice,
whacks back in its water, slams hard
at my line, but I keep it
all in good order, line taut, hand
on the reel turning, bringing the brown
to me, up along the shallow current,
no net so I'm into the water
scooping fish like a bear to the bank where
it flops wild on the grass in huge
gasps at my not quite delight
so awed by its hugeness, that it's here
the knots held, the fly stayed,
the big brown's here, on the grass
its golden belly, its scarlet spots
and blood from my finger, blood from its mouth
where I've broken its neck, both of us
settling down into silence
as the rain rages against the creek
chattering its newness in rushes
from beneath old ice, sending a new message
up and down its crooked capsizing length:

The big brown that lived
in the hole beneath the red willow
is gone, the man who fought it, took it,
bent over in silence, has
walked away, and the frogs, the minnows
have a day, a week, a season

of gliding free and easy
before another trout, not so big,
not so brown, moves in
to curve its jaw round every
swimming thing sliding down
the current to the dark hole
beneath the bowed red tree.

## RISING

Dear Auntie: I hear you're keeping watch over my dying uncle, the one I haven't seen in years, his changes would be drastic enough to you but

I can't be there to see this stranger in his murk of unknowing, the only grown-up to take me fishing, his brother my father being too jumpy, having little patience, but his brother your husband so quiet at Christmases I could hardly hear him speak, like a large river low and slowly moving, I have that one picture of us in your trailer somewhere in B.C., a trout I'd caught shining between us, the whiteness of our teeth spangling the picture my memory

now I'm his age, fishing, teaching my sons my granddaughters to fish, the studied flick of the wrist, the slow arc of line, distant splash dark form following steadily below the surface, now breaking through to flash silver, if he does, please tell him I've taken that one thing of his along
just that

## FOR ART, ON HIS WEDDING DAY

We drive up looking for fish
to the wind-washed valley you get
to call home, begging from your mother
her connections to people who know
the creeks, who might know
about fish. Dave tells your mother
he thinks the view out the front window
the best in the world, how lucky
she is to live here, and she knows it,
shares it with us over tea,
leads us to a creek in the hills.

I think back to how we got to know one another
walking a small road in the Kootenays
talking about women, about love, about
the cumbersome way we invade
the females' territory, not meaning
any harm, bewildered by the things
we sometimes say and do, stupefied
by their responses, and, as if
to emphasize my own basic stupidity
I waded into Mill Creek to grab
the spawning Kokanee salmon, held one
up for a picture, as if to say
look how easy it is to catch a fish,
look how deftly I can move,
how easily I can break the law,
interfere with the mating rituals
of a species that knows
exactly what it's doing.

As we walked that road in the shadow
of the towering clear-cut mountains
we likely wished for instincts
equally fearsome and direct,

but years of talking later
know only we obey the simple need to be
loved and loving, pushing aside
what gets in the way and moving
inexorably if fumblingly towards
whatever makes it work.

Dave and I at the end of that day
phone our wives to say we
found fish, we thanked our host,
that we'll be home soon. We mention
your name and what a great place
you come from, what a great start
instincts can have, and after that
how it's up to the same thing that guides
the fish, what tells us who to seek out
and love, what keeps us coming home,
praying for good days ahead.

## SYNECDOCHE

There on my filing cabinet, silly
white man snapshots of me holding
big fish — wide smile, the rod,
the old hat — are these what you call
trophies? Relation to those heads
and horns we saw on Hemingway's walls?

Each time I turn from the phone,
the pen, I catch sight
of those grinning men and their fish:
Big fish with me alone. One with my son
beside me. Big Craig Mitchell, what
a day that was. Just the sight
of us with those trout, the day
unspools before me: drive to Blackstrap,
crappy luck, packing up to
barrel 'cross country to Diefenbaker,
many casts, the yank and pull,
no net, the fight, Craig in water
to his knees hand-gaffing the impossible
rainbow to heave it
over the rocks. We
shared a smoke after that.
Laid out, panting on the shore.
Grinning like cub bears and my boy
getting out the camera
                    those photos
on my filing cabinet, silly
men in grins and old pants, days
and days of, yes, dead fish,
and my very best luck.

## THE BITTERN

A day later we ran across
a flock of partridge
a dozen of them in the ditch

and I couldn't get her
to see them, no matter
how I angled the car

but earlier as we drove
between sloughs I caught a glimpse
of a bittern

pulled a U-turn,
brought us up beside it
and it held, beak

to the sky, one eye
glaring in fear, believing itself
invisible among the sedge

and she saw it
her 91st birthday, started
reciting Sir Walter Scott

do you remember that poem?
she sang
I didn't, idling the car

watching her commune
with her alter-ego, camouflaged
and sharp-tipped

demure in church,
subdued before Dad's passion
offering always to bring baking

grandly eloquent now, ah,
the bittern she cried, proudly
reciting by the side of the road

## BENDING

Driving as far from city as I can
I take a room, rest, stare out my window
into sunlit afternoon of few people working
look for end of straight lines

sun behind projects roof above in black
upon grass makes perfect parallels
with sidewalk beyond

seven posts define parking lot
row of trees means end of lawn
but trees have grown imperfectly
weeds between attract weeds beyond

they run ragged over ditches leap streams
run crooked in the distance crooked
as my daydream broken by lawnmower
back curved over precise machinery
he smoothes ragged landscape
I fight him where I watch

think brave thoughts for the grasses
                                        for irregularities
of weeds

## NEWS FROM THE FIELDS

Amid piles of old newspapers we walk,
the tiny black words proclaiming black news,
all of it new as babies, old as hate.
In a world of words so much talk and talk
my foolish ardour would talk of you,
fill up blank pages with an urge to make
more words, piled up, more words to walk around,
so thrilled with my making, seduced by their sound.

With your fingers to your lips you stop me
making so many words I can't feel
and lead me from papers to the fields:

let all your talking be that lily
quietly ablaze in green grass
lone testament
                                        that in three days will pass.

## YOUR ENCOUNTER

At the cabin, the lake, the campground
we confront our selves, at least
that's the theory. Leave behind
the whirl of work and calls we've created
that convince ourselves we're alive, we
matter, have matter, occupy space and
machines in their multitude. We are.

In the woods, if we do it right,
or wrong, there are four walls and a calendar
dated last August, a toilet with a pail
or a hole in the ground, maybe some canvas
between you and the trees — okay
we've hiked, okay we've fished, swum,
picked berries, tried to fix the motor
so we can take the boat out and have
some real fun — now what? We sit
inside this little house that's not a house,
I said we may have done it wrong,
and we're sick of cards, finished
the lake book, the magazines
from last year. Now everything shuts down.
Now it's just you and you and God
Almighty is that . . . is that a bear walking
right through your yard? You didn't know
the blueberry crop is way down this year,
so now it's here to save you
from the fear of yourself. Do you
want fear? This fellow will do it. Yes,
he can eat you. Yes, he tore the neighbours'
outdoor freezer to pieces three nights ago.
To pieces. Now he's here. Right
outside your door. You're scared shitless.
Thank God. You've never been
so grateful.

## WHY I DIDN'T WANT YOU AT THE CABIN

no running water
   you think it's no big deal
   but after a few days
   of hauling it up from the lake
   heating it to do dishes, wash
   your face, an outdoor toilet
   I know it's not your kinda place

these cabin beds
   the bunks hard as boards
   the fold-out couch
                    in the front room
   the double with a sag
                    that destroys your back

the late-August weather
   that can be good
   but
again is windy, cold
   rain coming in the front screens
   it's hard even to go for a walk
   and how long can you
                    pick blueberries?

and fish, fish, fish
                    is that it?

Why I did want you
                    here now

is everything else

— *Little Bear Lake*

## BE(E)

that bee in the corner
buzzing crazy to get out
that's the part of me
                that knows
what I'd do with you
                given the chance

we talk, we sit
we move around
look at that bee, you say
get it out
before someone gets stung

and I do
    shoo it away
into the great wide sky

now there's just
        the two of us
what I say
what I mean

no angry buzzing
off to the side
unless that's something
we've yet to let out

## MOUSE IN THE HOUSE

This isn't really about the mouse,
is it? Though you hear it
behind your stove, think it
came over in the Christmas box
from your ex-husband's garage.

Angry with it, you say,
though you finally admit it's you
you're most angry with, scared
of a little furry thing, but
it's only being a mouse, isn't it?
37 below and driven indoors, it
isn't really the mouse but that other
creature that wants in, believing
he needs to be with your daughter,
thinking she was nice to him
once, phoning, peeking in
the windows.
So scared
you want to chase it down
step on it, squash it
with your boots, wearing them indoors
for such a purpose
squashing it dead under your sole
sick and angry at finding out
you could do such a thing.

## TRESPASSING

In a strange city
I feel empty
no property but my room key
a piece of metal
to open a space
I'm afraid to use.

I could take comfort
in the moon, nearly full,
but it doesn't feel like mine.
Just looking at it
I trespass.

In my small town I own
so much more of the moon
standing alone
with so few folk around
I can account
for all of them, know
none but me are holding
this globe of gold

and if someone approaches
I recognize him
remark on the moon
share my wealth.

— *Winnipeg*

## GILA MONSTERS IN THE RAIN

Another rainy day in the Forest City, me with runny nose, rainy eyes, capsized on a sea of tissues, strong tea, self-pity, groping through the only book that will make sense, a blue and white Field Guide, the beady-eyed snakes arrowed across the page, lumpy toads squatting like turds, the matter-of-factness of venom proclaims the world still as dangerous as I left it last night, as I woke to it this grey and bleary morning, just one hand up and over the wrong rock ledge in Colorado, Arizona, or sweet home Southern Ontario meets the accidental absolute of rattlesnake poised to strike, its mean triangular head afraid but not more than me, quickly turning the page to Gila Monster, club-tailed orange and black, the only venomous lizard, all my life I've lived convinced if I met one it would attack, its scary name dragging behind it like a club it can't outrun, the kind the Field Guide says not to use, the poor thing only expels poison when it chews, we can avoid it with good eyes and sturdy shoes just Leave The Poor Thing Alone the book warns or you'll wind up fined
in Arizona

What luck of all mornings to learn one thing less is out to get me. Let 'em come here to London if they like, these hapless lizards, live and let live I say, blow my nose, look at the sky turning blue as my Field Guide.

## WILD HEART

The city is an animal feeding off
the prairie around it building houses
and streets, throttling its energy
into building, building, maybe a few
drinks in buildings that can't contain
its wildness till it spills into the streets
and the cops are there, policing the beat
wild beat of the city's wild heart eating the fields
eating its own old houses and streets, frightened
deer breaking the windows of its suburban
defeat of wild grasses, lairs of animals
it meets, paving over opium dens,
speakeasies, barrelhouse kings
and queens the knife-wielding wildsters
who think they can beat the paved heart
building heart, black beat of the beast
that finds a cougar in its middle
shrieks in its grief: kill it, drug it,
drag it away, wild animal heart
in the heart of the city won't do, the only
wild heart in the city is you
and you and we've made laws to protect us
from those of us that is you, cheering
each of us in our homes now
for the cougar that is you
the cougar, a terror
by the river, last terror
cheered now, beaten down
that was you.

## CRICKETS

We met at a party — knew
each other from before but saw
one another with new eyes.
End of the night
I offered a ride home,
we drove into the black
of hilly prairie
where her family farmed, kept
a few cows, this kind of talk
rolling back and forth finding
where we were at either end
of the bench seat. Pulled in
the yard, up to the house.
Dad's home, she said, that's his truck,
look at him in the kitchen, the room
lit and throwing its light at us, across us,
bathing us clean of sweaty intention.
Watched him make and eat an onion
sandwich, she said he eats one
nearly every night. I wondered
how you could kiss someone after
an onion sandwich, but didn't wonder
aloud, just sat resolute behind the wheel
as my car ticked down cold
and the crickets started singing again
knowing I wasn't going anywhere soon
and they were safe to rub their legs.

## FULFILLED

*(Thinking of Don McKay's title* Birding, or Desire*)*

Imagine how simple this is.

You spot it in the slough
by the highway. You stop.
The cars and trucks thunder by.

You get out with your binoculars
and really get a look.
You're lucky. It sits there
in its rusty red body, its black

and white head, its outrageous
blue bill. It's amazing. The first
one you've seen.

Satisfied, you climb back up
the ditch, get in your truck,
drive away.

No shooting
No pictures
No stuffing and mounting

Despite the urge
to hold onto things beautiful
the most you do is write it down:
Ruddy Duck, 30 May '07, west of Mildred
an honour you were given
for noticing.

## OUR SCENIC WINDOW

The birds know nothing of yards,
property, what's made prices soar
with the rising wind. The merlin
takes down a house sparrow on
our front lawn, clump birch leaves just
coming in, picturesque beyond perennials
in the borders stretching back
into Spring. It tears
out the breast meat till a raven, all
humpy-beaked black swagger of it, pushes
its way into the feast, then it's the merlin,
nature red in tooth and claw, right at
our triple-glaze picture window. The raven
makes another move, the merlin takes
its prize up over the weeping carragana — did
it make it through the winter? — and the drama
moves on. No messy carcass on our just-
green lawn, the real estate returned
to its valuable splendour, a few small feathers
floating past our scenic window. Little birds
singing in the trees again like pretty birds
are supposed to do. What do birds know
of property? What's made prices soar
with the wind?

## FOUND BIRD

I found a bird on the street, green
with a yellow head caught
in my hand walked it home
put it on newspapers under
my laundry hamper where it scolded
my seeds my lid full of water

Phoned every one I could think of
left messages, it bit
my hand, scattered its seed

it was green like no green
I knew, black crow, dappled
magpie, tawny merlin, each one
willing to rip this one's skin off
if it didn't meet a cat.

Found a keeper with an extra cage
    drove it over
        job well done
phoned everyone back
left messages that lost
is found, settled anyway
till agencies open in the morning.

But still the calls came
    into the night
then six AM, seven, eight,
glad to hear the budgie's back
glad to hear you did right
glad to talk, tell me
thank you, I love
birds, and again
thank you till I had to say
enough
and shoo them off the phone.

## COMMUNITY

We're the oriole couple
hear the single clear note
the tentative, not-quite-declaration
and look up, backwards
                                        in circles
                    till we find it, little
smaller than a robin in the top
                    of the Manitoba maple
orange we can't pin
on the prairie lily, the pumpkin
that and the stark black, we say
to passersby who invariably stop
for a couple staring straight up.
They want to see, too
cat up a tree, kite, spaceship?
We point, say
                                        one limb over
                    just above the wire
                    there, size
                    nearly of a robin
that orange, they say
thank us for pointing it out
for including them